Ancient Myths: The First Science Fiction

by
Laurence and Irene Swinburne

Published by

Distributed exclusively by

RAINTREE CHILDRENS BOOKS
Milwaukee • Toronto • Melbourne • London

St. Joseph, Michigan

Library of Congress Number: 77-10915

Art Credits

Cover illustration by Lynn Sweat
Illustrations on pages 6, 10, 12, 13, 15, 16, 18, 22, 24, 27, 29, 31, 34, 35, 37, 38, 41, 45, and 47, by Mary Kornblum.
Every effort has been made to trace the ownership of all copyrighted material in the book and to obtain permission for its use.

Library of Congress Cataloging in Publication Data

Swinburne, Laurence,
   Ancient myths: the first science fiction

   CONTENTS: Heracles and the many-sided snake.—Perseus and the helmet of invisibility.—Orpheus' journey under the Earth.—The man who couldn't be hurt.
   1. Mythology, Greek—Juvenile literature. [1. Mythology, Greek] I. Swinburne, Irene, joint author. II. Title.
PZ8.1.S9545An 292'.1'3 [398.2] 77-10915
ISBN 0-8172-1042-3 lib. bdg.

Manufactured in the United States of America.
ISBN 0-8172-1042-3

Contents

Chapter 1
   Heracles and the Many-Headed Snake   7

Chapter 2
   Perseus and the Helmet of Invisibility   17

Chapter 3
   Orpheus' Journey Under the Earth   30

Chapter 4
   The Man Who Couldn't Be Hurt   39

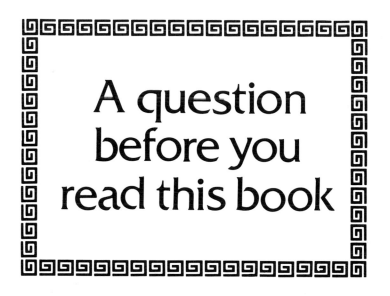

A question before you read this book

In this book are some famous ancient myths about what might be the world's earliest *bionic people*. At the end of each story, you will see how today's science fiction writers have "borrowed" from the ancient myth. Clues are hidden in the stories. For example, Heracles, the strongest man in the first Greek myth in this book, is most like our present-day "Six-Million-

Dollar" Bionic Man. Can you figure out who Perseus is most like? How about Achilles? Only one thing could weaken his power. Doesn't that remind you of a "mild-mannered reporter" for the *Daily Planet*?

See if you can figure out which modern hero is most like the heroes of the ancient myths.

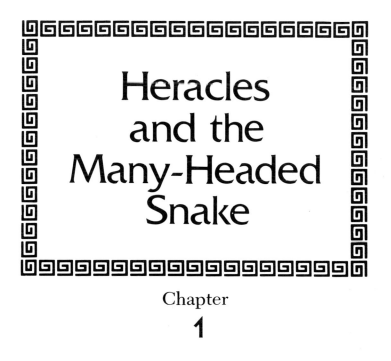

Heracles
and the
Many-Headed
Snake

Chapter

1

King Eurystheus stared at the huge man who seemed to fill half the throne room. How he hated this giant!

"You have finished just one of your tasks, Heracles," the King roared, "although I cannot understand how you accomplished it. But you still have nine more. Have you forgotten?"

7

"I remember," said Heracles lazily. "How could I forget the punishment of the gods? What is next, Eurystheus? I would like to do them as quickly as possible, so I can leave this miserable court."

The King's cheek turned red with anger. "Can you show me no respect?"

Eurystheus bit his lip to control his temper. Then he broke into a smile, but it had no warmth behind it. "I have a wonderful task for you, one that will test all your courage and cunning. You must kill the Great Hydra!"

Heracles did his best not to show his feelings, but Eurystheus knew the giant did not like the command. Heracles turned and hurried from the throne room in silence. A young boy followed the large man outside. The boy's name was Iolaüs. He was the nephew of Heracles.

"Why are you rushing away?" asked Iolaüs. "You promised me that you would take me on your next mission. What is the Great Hydra?"

Heracles looked grim. "I have never seen the creature, but all I have heard is frightening. It is a powerful snake that lives in a swamp."

Iolaüs frowned, not understanding. "But you have killed large snakes before."

"This is no ordinary snake, nephew. It is a mile long. The Hydra poisons the very air it breathes. And it has nine heads! One of its heads can never die. Now you see why I cannot take you. I may not come back myself."

Iolaüs thought. "You promised me, uncle," he said at last, "and it is well known that Heracles never breaks a promise."

The giant sighed. "That is true and I can see you mean to hold me to it. Very well, come along. You may even be of some small help. All I hope is that your mother will forgive me for this!"

They rode in a chariot pulled by two wild horses across deserts and over mountains. For three days they traveled, only stopping to rest and eat. Finally, they reached the swamp of Lerna, the home of the dreaded Hydra.

The rest of the journey was on foot. As they went deeper and deeper into the wooded swamp, the shadows of the twisted ugly trees became darker. The cold and slimy mud crawled up their legs.

Finally, they reached the heart of the swamp. There rose before them a large hill with a cave dug into it.

Iolaüs looked fearfully into the dark mouth of the cave. "Do we go in, Heracles?"

Heracles and Iolaüs set out to find the hideous Hydra.

His uncle shook his head. "It's bad enough that we have to face the Great Hydra on its own ground. I don't want to fight it in its own home." He quickly shot three arrows into the cave. There was a roar and the Great Hydra crawled out.

Iolaüs drew back in horror. The enormous snake rose high above them, its nine heads spitting and hissing. The boy would have run if he hadn't been frozen with fear. And, of course, he was with the powerful Heracles! Besides, he didn't dare move. The last thing in the world he would do was shame himself in front of his uncle —a great Greek hero.

Heracles went right to work. His mighty club came down on one head and then another and then another.

But each time he knocked off one of the Hydra's heads, two more grew in its place! Finally, there were three times as many heads as there had been before. Heracles was getting tired! Sooner or later, the monster would crush him to death.

"Iolaüs, are you still there?" called Heracles, not daring to turn around to see.

Just as Heracles would knock off one head,
another head would appear.

The boy was standing at the edge of the clearing. Although frightened, he was still thrilled by his uncle's strength. He watched with pride as Heracles knocked off the heads. No one in the whole world was half as strong as his mighty Uncle Heracles!

"I can't last much longer," panted the huge man. "Find a thick tree branch and light it."

Iolaüs whipped out his knife and slashed at the nearest tree. Its half-rotted branches came off easily. In a few moments, the thickest branch was flaming. Iolaüs crept up behind Heracles.

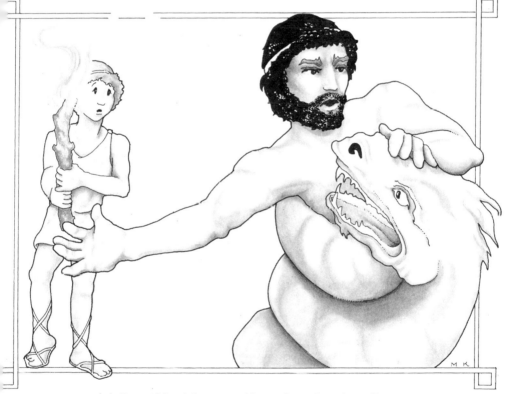

Iolaüs grabbed the rotted branch and set it on fire.

Heracles, struggling in the coils of the big snake, held out his free hand. He didn't say a word as he took the burning wood. He knocked off another head with his club. Before two heads could grow in its place, he thrust the fire into the open wound.

Iolaüs gave a cry of joy. No head had appeared. The heat had sealed the wound as tightly as if it had been sewed with strong rope. With this victory, Heracles' strength seemed to return. He swung his club at one head after another. After a head fell off, he sealed the wound.

At last, all the snake's heads lay on the ground. The body of the once-great monster fell in a heap.

Cheering, Iolaüs ran towards the hero. As he passed one of the snake heads, it tried to bite his heel. Before the fangs were about to close on the boy's heel, Heracles snatched his nephew out of danger.

"That's the head that cannot die!" Leaning down, Heracles scooped out a hole. Angrily, he kicked the head in the hole and covered it with a rock that was as large as a man.

Heracles had to bury the Hydra head that wouldn't die.

"You truly are the *strongest man* in the world," said Iolaüs. He looked down in wonder at the Hydra's dead body.

His uncle laughed. "Maybe so. But I can tell you one thing, lad. I never could have killed this monster without your help!"

A wise, strong hero and his young helper use their wits as well as their strength to wipe out evil. Does this "deadly duo" remind you of any modern-day team of heroes?

Our next tale may also bring to mind a modern-day myth—a hero with the power to make himself *invisible* before the very eyes of his awful enemies.

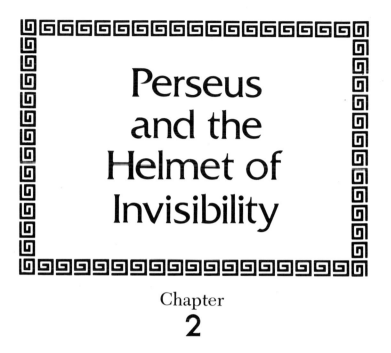

Perseus and the Helmet of Invisibility

Chapter
2

King Polydectes was planning to be married —or so he said. He wouldn't tell anyone the name of his bride. People from all over the kingdom brought him wedding gifts. All but one youth, Perseus, who was a servant of the King.

"What? You brought me no gift, Perseus?" The crafty King smiled at the young man.

"I would bring you a present, great King," said Perseus, his face growing red, "but I have no money to buy one."

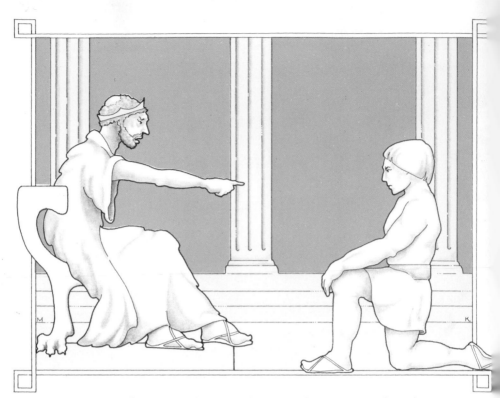

Perseus was too embarrassed to look into the
eyes of King Polydectes.

The King looked around at the members of
his court. "Think of that! He has no money!
Why, he says he is the grandson of King Acrisius
across the sea. He also says his father was Zeus,
leader of all the gods. Yet this half-man, half-god
has not even the money for a small gift!"

"All that is true, Polydectes," said Perseus,
looking around at the shocked faces of the group

18

gathered around the King. "You have heard my mother say it."

"Ah, yes, the fair Danaë! Listen, everyone, do you know how they came to this land, this boy and his mother? My brother, Dictys, was fishing and found a large box floating on the sea. He opened it and, lo and behold, there were Danaë and Perseus. This happened a few years ago when this great hulk of a youth was only a baby. Now, does a large box seem like a boat fit for a queen?"

"You know the reason for that," said the now angry Perseus. "My grandfather was told by a fortune-teller that I would someday kill him and take the throne. That is why he had my mother and me thrown into the sea."

All the onlookers began to understand what Polydectes was doing. Like a snake weakening a small animal before eating it, the King was leading Perseus into a trap.

"If it were in my power, I would get you a present, Polydectes!" Perseus shouted. "You know I would." Perseus was so ashamed his eyes welled with hot tears.

"Perhaps it *is* in your power," purred the older man. "I want the head of the Gorgon Medusa!"

Everyone around Perseus gasped. They knew the King had finally sprung his trap. There were three Gorgons—horrible creatures, part-human and part-bird. Their bodies were covered with scales and their faces were hideous. Their claws were long and sharp as knives. The ugliest was Medusa. She had snakes on her head instead of hair. Anyone who looked at her turned to stone. But before anyone could stop him, the angry, embarrassed youth cried out for all to hear, "I will do it. You shall have the head of the Gorgon Medusa!"

When Perseus told his mother that evening of his promise to bring back the head, she was beside herself. "Don't you see what Polydectes did and why he did it?" Danaë asked. "You are tall and strong. You have won so many wrestling matches and races that the young men look up to you. Polydectes is afraid you will sweep him from the throne."

But it was too late. The promise had been made, and the son of Zeus always kept a promise. Perseus started on his trip, not knowing where he might find the Gorgons. He was sure he would come across them sooner or later. He had gotten just a few miles from the palace when a tall woman stepped out of the woods and stood before him. "Who are you?" Perseus asked in alarm.

She smiled gently at him. "I am Athene, also a child of Zeus. Don't be afraid. I've come to help you. You must never give up hope for that is really what it means to be brave."

The tall woman came closer. "You must go into the woods, my brother. There you will find the home of three witches. They know where there are three weapons that can conquer the Gorgons."

The woods were dark and gloomy, but Perseus had no trouble finding a path that led to an old house. He peered in through a window. There, three hags were sitting around a table. On the table was a beautiful gem.

With a start, Perseus realized that two of the old women had no eyes, and the third had only one eye. He listened at the window as they spoke.

21

The witches took turns looking at the shining stone.

"Give me the eye, sister," complained one of the blind witches. "You've had it long enough. It's my turn to look at the shining stone now."

As the one-eyed witch removed the eye, Perseus had an idea. He sprang through the window and pulled the eye from the witch's hand. "I will return this eye only if you tell me where to find what I must know. Where are the three weapons to use against the Gorgons?"

The blind witches knew they were trapped. They had to have their eye back. "The wood nymphs have the weapons," said one of the witches. "Go back through the woods on the path. When you leave the forest, you will be in a wide field. In the center of the field is a small grove of trees. That's the home of the wood nymphs. Now give us the eye!"

He threw it on the table. Then he slipped out the same way he came and made his way through the woods. Soon he approached the grove of the nymphs. They were half-humans, half-spirits in the form of lovely young women. Ten of them sat around a pool within the grove. As Perseus approached them, they screamed and began to run.

"Don't go," he called gently. "I don't wish you any harm. Athene sent me."

They stopped running when they heard the goddess's name. But they kept their distance. "What do you want?" one frightened nymph asked in a voice that sounded like music.

"Athene said you had three weapons that would help me to fight the Gorgons."

The nymph's eyes grew wide. Why would anyone be so foolish as to fight the Gorgons? But in less than a moment she brought Perseus a helmet, a pair of shoes, and a shield. The young man could hardly believe his eyes. "Athene must be playing a joke on me. I have these already."

The nymphs gave Perseus a magic helmet, a pair of shoes, and a magic shield.

"Oh, but not like these," sang the nymph. "Look at the wings on these shoes. They will carry you to the rocky island in the middle of the sea. You can reach the Gorgons in no other way. They always stay on a cliff ledge. And this shield —what do you see when you look at it?"

Perseus stared at the shield. "Why, my own face! It's as shiny as a mirror. Why would a shield be made that way?"

"So the Gorgons will see their own faces," answered the nymph with a smile.

"I understand." Perseus pointed to the last weapon. "But the helmet looks like any other helmet."

"Put it on," said the nymph.

As soon as Perseus put the helmet on, he could no longer see his body. "What has happened? My body has disappeared!"

"The helmet has made you invisible," said the nymph. "Good luck, Perseus."

Perseus thanked her, strapped on the shining shield, and then put on the shoes. Carrying the helmet, he was suddenly lifted into the air, and he was soon flying over the wide sea.

As he came near the rocky island, he could see the Gorgons sleeping in the afternoon sun. He knew he didn't dare look directly at their faces for he would turn to stone. He steered himself down toward the Gorgons by watching them in the mirror of the shield. He saw Medusa lying in the middle. He knew her because of the snakes she had in place of hair. How ugly she was! Perseus placed the helmet on his head and immediately became invisible.

With his sword, the unseen Perseus cut cleanly through Medusa's neck. He seized the sleeping snakes and dropped the head into a cloth bag.

As Perseus flew away, the other two Gorgons woke. When they saw Medusa's headless body, they screeched in fury. They rose from their ledge and flew about looking for their sister's killer. Of course, they could not see Perseus because he was invisible.

Perseus returned the shield, shoes, and helmet to the nymphs. They would keep them until

The ugly Medusa was no match for Perseus.

another hero came along to borrow them for a great adventure.

When he came near Polydectes' palace, he found a man sitting on a rock. It was Dictys. He was startled to see the brave young man.

"Perseus! Everyone thinks you are dead. Polydectes is forcing your mother to marry him.

That is one of the reasons he wanted you out of the way. He feared you would stop him. I have loved your mother since I found you two floating in that box in the sea."

Perseus remembered the words of Athene and said, "Never give up hope, Dictys. That is true bravery! Come on, *we're going to a wedding!*"

The throne room was filled with people. Perseus, followed by Dictys, pushed his way through the crowd until he reached the proud King. Danaë stood weeping by Polydectes' side.

The King's face was a mixture of fear and fury when he saw Perseus. "Take this fool and throw him in the deepest dungeon!" he shouted at his soldiers.

Perseus laughed. "You mean you want to get rid of me before you see the wedding gift I have brought you?" He snatched Medusa's head from the bag and shoved it before Polydectes' face.

Polydectes immediately turned to stone. Perseus dropped the "gift" back into the bag and kissed his mother.

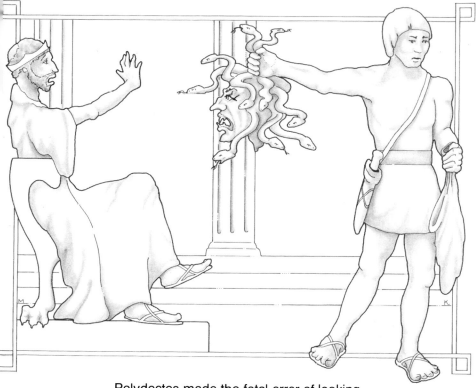
Polydectes made the fatal error of looking
at the head of Medusa.

There was a wedding that day . . . between
Danaë and Dictys. Everyone wanted Perseus to
become king, but he refused. "Dictys is far wiser
than I am and better fitted to sit on the throne.
Besides, I am young and still have a lot of adven-
tures ahead of me and a lot of the world to see."

*Could our hero, Perseus, be one of many he-
roes of our modern myths? A hero who can make
himself invisible to others!*

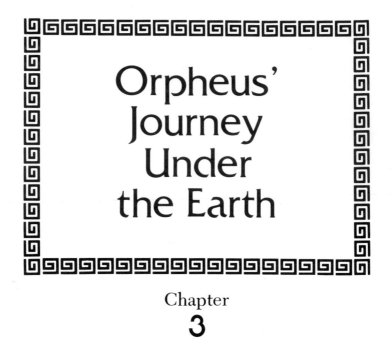

Orpheus' Journey Under the Earth

Chapter
3

There is no doubt that Orpheus was the finest singer who ever lived. All the gods and humans agreed on that point. Once he touched the strings of his harp—or *lyre*, as it was called—everyone would stop and listen. Even the rocks and the trees danced to his songs.

One reason Orpheus could produce such beautiful music was his harp. It had been given to Orpheus by Apollo, his father and the god of the sun. Ah, but Orpheus' voice! *That* was all his own.

All the women loved Orpheus. But his love was given to only one. The first time he saw Eurydice, he knew he had to marry her. It did not take her long to accept his offer. But their

The beautiful Eurydice didn't see the snake in the swamp.

happiness was too great to last forever. Not long after the wedding, Eurydice stepped on a snake in the high grass near a river. Startled, the snake bit her with its poisonous fangs. In a matter of minutes, Eurydice was dead.

Orpheus was shocked by what had happened. His lovely Eurydice dead! For a time he would not sing or play. Sad and lonely, Orpheus felt his own life was over. The god of death, Hades, had Eurydice somewhere and Orpheus had to have her back. Finally, a day came when Orpheus announced that, whatever the cost, he would find his wife and bring her back.

His friends could hardly believe their ears. Orpheus must have gone crazy, they thought.

"You can't do that," they argued. "Hades would never let her go. Hades will keep you there, Orpheus! No one has gone down to Tartarus and returned," they warned.

Orpheus could only reply, "I must go. Life is nothing without her. What difference will it make if Hades will not let me return?"

Nothing anyone said could change his mind. As all Greeks of those days knew, the dead went to Tartarus, a land far beneath the earth. This gloomy place was ruled by the god Hades. They knew the tunnel that led to Tartarus. But no human, until now, ever went willingly into it . . . no human except Orpheus.

"Wish me luck," he said to his friends as he stood at the entrance. They wished him the best. He smiled for the first time since Eurydice's death, but it was a sad smile.

Waving goodbye, he entered the tunnel. His friends could hear his harp playing. They heard him sing his most beautiful songs. They stood there for a long time until the last echoes of Orpheus' songs died away.

Orpheus walked a long time in the dark until he reached the River Styx. There, a boatman looked angrily at the visitor. This was Charon who rowed the dead across to Tartarus. But as soon as Charon had heard Orpheus' song, he smiled and led the way to the boat.

Orpheus passed through many rooms filled with the dead. There were great heroes and even greater cowards. There were lovers who, like Eurydice, died too early. There were old kings and queens and ordinary people who had

Charon, the boatman of the River Styx, led Orpheus to Hades.

passed on. All stopped whatever they were doing to listen to Orpheus' songs.

Finally, Orpheus entered the great, dark throne room. There sat Hades and his queen, Persephone. Orpheus sang for the fearsome keepers of the dead. His song told them of his

34

deep love for Eurydice and her love for him. He reminded them of when they were young and how much in love they had been. At last, he stopped. He had done his best, and he could sing no more. He waited for the verdict.

Finally, Hades spoke. "No one has ever come here and returned to the sunshine of the

Orpheus played his harp and sang for Hades and Persephone.

earth. But your singing has touched the hearts of my wife and myself. Eurydice is freed. She will follow you up to the surface. But listen carefully, Orpheus. You must not look around, not even once, to see if she is there. *Mark my words well!*"

Orpheus thanked them and departed. He went once again through the halls of the dead. He passed over the River Styx.

All the way, he was tempted to turn around and look back. He could not hear any footsteps. Could it be that Hades and Persephone had lied to him?

Finally, just a few steps from the entrance to the upper world, he could stand it no more. He turned. Just behind him he saw a woman dressed in gray, her face hidden by a hood.

"Oh, Orpheus," said the figure in a sad voice. He knew at once it was Eurydice. "You could not wait. Now I must return below."

Before his very eyes, she vanished!

Orpheus was never happy again. He finally died and his body was thrown into a river. As it

Orpheus disobeyed the order of Hades. He turned
to look at Eurydice.

floated down the stream, the dead lips kept say-
ing, "Eurydice, Eurydice!"

The gods did not forget Orpheus, though.
They buried him at the foot of Mount Olympus,
a place of great honor.

*We can't come up with a super-hero of today
who seems much like Orpheus. There is a hero*

of a myth known by children all over the world. That hero used his beautiful music to help a town get rid of its rat problem. Remember the hero's name?

Our last story deals with a hero whose strength was so great he could not be hurt in any way—except one.

The Man
Who Couldn't
Be Hurt

Chapter

4

As you have now seen, the course of love in these ancient myths doesn't always run smoothly. For every story that has a happy ending, such as Perseus saving his mother, there is one, like Orpheus and Eurydice, that ends sadly. This last story is a mixture of happiness and sadness. The marriage is a happy one, but someone else is hurt by it.

Peleus, a human, fell in love with Thetis, a goddess who lived under the sea most of the time. Usually such a match was frowned upon by the gods of Mount Olympus. Somehow, though, they didn't mind this one. In fact, all the gods came to the wedding which was held in the cave of a *centaur*, a creature that was half-man and half-horse.

A son was born to this marriage. Peleus and Thetis named the boy Achilles. Like so many Greeks who had gods or goddesses for parents, Achilles would become a hero. But Achilles was a human, and so he would die sooner or later. His mother worried about this. She wanted him to live a long life. She knew that he probably would be a warrior. And warriors are often killed in battle.

When Achilles was just a few days old, she carried him down the long tunnel Orpheus took to Tartarus. But she only went as far as the River Styx. Charon, the boatman, was startled.

"He looks too healthy to be coming here, Thetis," he said.

"And healthy I want him to stay for a very long time," Thetis said. "I only want to dip him in the Styx. I have heard that that will protect him from harm. Is that right?"

Charon smiled. "That's true. Go right ahead."

Thetis held her child by the back of his foot and quickly dipped him into the dark waters. She lifted him out and lay the crying baby in a blanket.

Thetis dipped Achilles into the River Styx.

Achilles grew into a strong young man. He was always the winner at games and races. He could use a sword more skillfully than others of his age. Even as a little boy, he could throw a spear farther than his father. He had a deadly aim with a bow and arrow. And he could tame the wildest horses. He only seemed to have one fault, a very quick temper. But none of his friends minded this. Nor were they jealous about his fighting skills.

Achilles' best friend, Patroclus, was always praising him. They were always together. How could Achilles know that someday he would cause the death of Patroclus?

Soon after Achilles became a man, the Trojan War broke out. Paris, one of the sons of the Trojan king, had kidnapped Helen, wife of the King of Greece. Hundreds of Greek ships set out for the city of Troy. Thousands of Greek soldiers vowed revenge.

There were many heroes in the Greek army. Achilles was the greatest hero. He was admired as a leader. Many young men like his friend Patroclus followed him into war.

The war between the Greeks and the Trojans lasted ten years. Alternately, the

Trojans or the Greeks would win important battles. When everything seemed hopeless for one side, the tables would be turned. Even the gods took sides.

The greatest of the Trojan heroes was Hector. Unlike his brother Paris, he was a fair and honest man. He was even respected by the Greeks.

Often it was the courage of Hector that kept the Greeks from winning. Just as often, it was Achilles who turned defeat into victory for the Greeks.

The leader of the whole Greek army was Agamemnon—a brave man and a good fighter. He and Achilles didn't like each other from the first time they met. They were both proud warriors and both had the same quick temper. It was only a matter of time before they would have an argument. When it finally came, it was a big one. The two men might have fought it out with swords if it hadn't been for the other Greek leaders.

Achilles had the last word. "Fight this war yourself!" he shouted. He and his warriors withdrew to a hill where they could see everything and "sit out" the war.

Soon the Trojans came out of the city, swords drawn and spears high. They were led, as usual, by Hector. Some say he fought that day like Ares, the war god. Before long, the Greek army was in full retreat, fleeing toward their ships.

Achilles would watch none of this. He sat in his tent, still full of fury at Agamemnon. But his men were watching outside. Suddenly, Patroclus rushed into the tent. "Achilles, we are losing. In only a few minutes, the war will be over if something is not done. The Greeks who survive will be sailing back across the sea."

"I don't care," said young Achilles.

"Well, I do," said Patroclus hotly. "I want to go, but I can't if you don't let me. You're my leader."

"Go then," said Achilles. "Use my armor if you wish. I won't need it."

When the fleeing Greeks saw the warriors come down the hill, they took heart. And when they saw the armor of the leader, they thought that Achilles had come back. They forced the Trojans to a halt.

Patroclus, wearing the armor of Achilles, was killed by Hector.

But Patroclus was killed by Hector. When a messenger brought the news to Achilles, he burst into tears. He knew it was his fault that his friend had died. He swore he would avenge this death.

Achilles charged into the battle. He was like a human storm, his spear stabbing this way, jabbing that way. The Greeks found new strength and followed his lead.

The Trojans fought bravely for a while, but their cause became hopeless. They could do nothing to stop the determined Greeks. The Trojan army turned and ran for their home city.

Achilles caught up to Hector before the Trojan leader could enter the gates of Troy. It was not a long struggle. Hector went down, his neck cut by Achilles' spear.

The long battle was over. Achilles tied Hector's leg to his chariot and drove around the city walls dragging the body behind him. There could be no worse insult to the enemy! Achilles gave Patroclus a beautiful funeral while the body of Hector was left lying outside his tent.

Priam, Hector's aged father and King of Troy, came to the Greek lines under a truce. He begged Achilles to let him take home the body of the Trojan hero. Achilles' fury left him. He thought about how his mother and father would feel if it were his body lying outside Hector's tent. Achilles let Priam take the body home. It was not long afterward that Paris vowed revenge for his brother Hector's death. He had to destroy Achilles—but *how*?

Paris had heard the story of how Thetis had dipped her baby Achilles into the waters of the Styx.

"But she held him by the heel of his foot," he said to himself. "His heels couldn't have touched the water."

Paris sneaked up behind Achilles and shot him in the heel of his foot with a poison arrow.

Paris shot an arrow into Achilles' heel.

Paris knew that this was the one part of Achilles' body that could be harmed. It was, indeed, the one part that the magical water had not touched.

So it was that the great Achilles died.

Achilles, the Greek hero who nothing—almost nothing—could harm was finally brought down by his one weak spot. Can you think of a popular modern hero, all-powerful except for one weakness?

By the way, the heroes of modern myths we thought matched the ancient heroes were:

Heracles and Iolaüs—*"Batman and Robin"*
Perseus—*"The Invisible Man"* or *"The Shadow"*
Orpheus—*"The Pied Piper"*
Achilles—*"Superman"* (his weakness is
         Kryptonite)